All the Things I Did Today

by Enrique Flores

illustrated by Celine Malpary

Harcourt

Orlando   Boston   Dallas   Chicago   San Diego

Visit *The Learning Site!*
www.harcourtschool.com

It's morning.
I wake up.

I eat my breakfast.
I drink my juice.

I put things in my
backpack.
I say good-bye.

I run to the bus stop.
I get on the bus.

I say hello to my
friends.

I paint a picture.
I read a story.

It's afternoon.
I go home on the bus.

I visit my friend.
I do my homework.

It's night.
I have dinner with
my family.

I put on my pajamas.
I brush my teeth.

I listen to a story.
I fall asleep.
Goodnight!